WORLD COSTUMES

116

SWEDEN

WORLD COSTUMES

BY

ANGELA BRADSHAW

WITH SIXTEEN PLATES IN COLOUR
AND
ONE HUNDRED AND FORTY-TWO PAGES OF DRAWINGS

LONDON
ADAM AND CHARLES BLACK

FIRST PUBLISHED 1952
REPRINTED 1954 AND 1959
A. & C. BLACK LTD.
4, 5 & 6 SOHO SQUARE
LONDON WI

To

F.B. AND A.B.

MADE IN GREAT BRITAIN
PRINTED BY MORRISON AND GIBB LTD., LONDON AND EDINBURGH

CONTENTS

Introduction	9–14
Abyssinia	17–18
Africa	19–22, 60, 123
Albania	23
America, United States	24–26
Anatolia	27
Arabia	28–29
Armenia	30
Assam	31
Australia	32
Austria *	33–37
Bolivia	38
Borneo	39–40
British West Indies	101–103
Burma *	41–45
Cambodia	47
Ceylon	48–49
China	50, 64, 160–161
Czechoslovakia *	51–55
Denmark	56–57
Dutch East Indies	58–59
East Africa	22
Egypt	60
Ecuador	61
Esthonia	62
Finland	63
Formosa	64
France	65–68
Germany *	69–75
Ghana	20
Greece	76–77
Greenland	78–79
Holland	80–82
Hungary	83–85
India *	31, 86–95
Indo-China—Cambodia	47
Indonesia	58–59
Ireland	96
Italy	97–100
Jamaica *	101–103
Japan *	104–108
Java	58–59
Kashmir	94
Korea	109–110
Kurdistan	111–112
Labrador	113
Lapland	114
Latvia	115
Madagascar	21
Mexico *	116–119
Mongolia *	120–121
Morocco	123
Natal	20
Nepal	86, 89
Nigeria	19
Norway	124

* indicates that a colour plate of the costume of this country is included

PERSIA	III–II2, I25	SPAIN	I5I–I52
PERU	126	SUDAN	21
PHILIPPINES	127	SWEDEN *	I53–I57
POLAND *	I28–I3I	SWITZERLAND	I58–I59
PORTUGAL *	I32–I35		
		TIBET	I60–I6I
ROUMANIA	I36–I39	TURKESTAN *	163
RUSSIA *	30, 62, II5, I40–I47	TURKEY	27
SARDINIA	97–98	UGANDA	22
SCOTLAND	148	UNITED STATES OF AMERICA	24–26
SIAM	I49–I50		
SIBERIA *	145	WALES	162
SICILY	99	WEST AFRICA	I9, 20, 22
SOUTH AFRICA (NATAL)	20	YUGOSLAVIA *	I65–I70

ANCIENT COSTUME

ANCIENT EGYPTIAN	I73	ETRUSCAN	I74
BABYLONIAN	I73	BYZANTINE	I75
ANCIENT HEBREW	I73	DACIAN	I75
ANCIENT PERSIAN	I73	CELTIC	I75
ANCIENT GREEK	I73	ANCIENT GAUL	I75
ROMAN	I74		

ENGLISH COSTUME

NORMAN	178	1650	I85–I86
I350	I78–I79	1675	187
I400	180	1700	188
I450	180, 181	1780	189
I500	182	1800	190
I550	183	1815	190
I600	184	1850	191
I640	185	1900	191

INTRODUCTION

WITH its examples of traditional dress in most parts of the world, this book's aim is to provide a general work of reference and to assist the artist and designer in search of stimulation and new ideas.

Many of the costumes illustrated here are still worn to-day and in some cases they have not changed for several centuries, so proving that the dress is the one most suited to its environment. Initially the dress of a people is determined by the climate and by the natural materials available. At a later stage social and religious demands and individual ingenuity may modify it, and if the community is not an isolated one external influences may alter and even cause the native dress to disappear from everyday use, to be worn only on festivals and holidays. Inevitably there is a similarity in the shape and cut of costumes worn in the same sort of environment, and often it is left to decoration to give a distinctive national or local individuality. The importance of decoration in costume cannot be over-emphasised, for it reveals with freedom and natural charm many aspects of the life and customs of a country and its people. Decoration frequently has a symbolic significance; birds, beasts and flowers are common sources of inspiration and the diverse ways in which they can be used according to the impulse of a religious or social influence are shown in many examples in this book. The sun, the stars, the moon and clouds are reproduced in decorative form in many parts of the world, and sometimes the geographical position of a country may be mirrored in designs. Island races and those with a sea-coast may reflect the surrounding seas in colour, and in decorative symbols such as scales, shells, seaweed, sea-horses, sea-birds and serpents in many different forms. The water symbol, with its offspring, the wave, fret and key patterns, may be inspired by the sea, a river, floods or deluge. Sometimes tribes from forest lands decorate their costumes with representations of their flora and fauna; while deserts and mountain peaks also lend their inspiration.

Climatic conditions often dominate the colours chosen for embroidered, woven or painted decoration. The brown Kutch, the gorse-yellow tumeric and the earth redlac of India, the cochineal of Mexico, the dark indigos, the making of which entranced Marco Polo, the bright reds, earth browns, yellows and non-fugitive colours used where the sunlight is particularly strong, and the soft glowing shades of the Persian gardens all have had a strong influence on the decoration and ornamentation of costume.

Traditional dress was and is still in many regions of the world dependent largely upon local resources. In the great sheep-rearing districts the materials used were wool and sheepskins ; silk was used where the silk-worm was reared, and in mountain regions goats' hair. In ice-lands reindeer skins and felt from beàten horsehair, oil, milk and dung. Felt cloth was also made from the bark of trees. Where other material was scarce straw and grasses were worn often matted or plaited. In countries where trade developed and industry thrived fine linens, silks, velvets, damasks, brocades, muslins, lace and cotton material were used. Where the resources of a country were poor, and exchange in trade was slow, bones, seeds, animals' teeth, tusks, ivory, discs, beads and shells were used in personal adornment.

The development of the town, opportunities for travel and the expansion of commerce between countries through the centuries introduced new ideas to the peasant and enlarged his expressive powers, and with the introduction of printing, illustrated books became the means of a more rapid and wider distribution of ideas.

The Crusades brought new ideas from the East ; the small pouch of the Arab was quickly converted by the ladies of the West into an embroidered bag hanging from the waist to hold money, thread and needles, and has often appeared in peasant costume. Worsted, linen, woollen goods and amber were taken eastwards by the Crusaders, and on the return journey the men brought back damasks, velvets, silks, fine linens, leather goods and the thin strip weaving of the Oriental craftsmen.

Islam has left its influence, in the small intricate patterns of Spain, and in the confite weave of Sicily and Calabria. The Arab word *Magramah*, too, now preserved in the word Macramé, a cord work which is much used by the peasants, suggests the influence of Islam, and it is also seen in soft colours, such as the Galician blues, and the golden browns and gorse yellows of Toledo and Avila.

The old caravan routes of the early steppe people led along the Pe Lu road over the Gobi ànd along the hills to Kashgar and through the plains to Iran and the Nan Lu road from the Gobi to Khotan and Yarkand where the tamarisks grow. Along these routes, dress has not changed much since the time of the Mongol Temujin, when they wore thick quilted coats, skin trousers, short felt boots and wide leather belts. Their women wore long quilted coats, binding round them blue scarves and wearing over their baggy sheepskin trousers high leather boots with gaily painted wooden heels. Their faces were greased and protected by long flowing veils, their hair was worn high, shaved across the forehead and sometimes covered by a diadem of flowers. This form of head-dress can be traced later to countries invaded by the Mongol people of the steppe. These styles were seen particularly in Russia where a girl's hair was coiled over birch frames and then intertwined with fresh or artificial flowers. The Shapka, the fur or woollen cap worn by the men and the thick felt boots or lapti, plaited birch-bark shoes, show the influence of the steppe. The cozhuh coat, with its traditional ornament of cut-leather designs, followed closely the decoration of the *szür* of Hungary and the applied leatherwork on the clothes of the Mongols.

The head-dresses, the kokochniks, kikas and povoiniks showed very strong Mongol influence, especially with their wide veils, fatas, often exquisitely embroidered. The peasant women's costume from Tula, with its peculiar fringed head-dress with long beaded tassels falling to the shoulders, the tunic with sleeves and shoulders thickly embroidered in braid and the bead collars all show strong Asiatic influence. In Smolensk, the extremely long sleeves into which the hands could be slipped in cold weather were reminiscent of Mongolian styles. The peculiar head-dress of Riazon is similar to that once worn by the Reindeer Tunguses from Siberia, and the cross-over tunic, composed of thin woven strips so that the whole effect appears striped, is similar to the costume of the Uzbeg women of Turkestan. Some embroidery on the costumes of Bohemia, though not showing much evidence of Mongol occupation, may be based on folk-lore with its tales of Mongol terror; the flying horses featured so much in Bohemian design almost certainly were derived from the Mongol ponies. Certain jackets which the women occasionally wore, with small basques, were similar to those worn by the Lithuanians. These jackets were of Tartar origin and could be found wherever an Asiatic race had settled in the West.

The decorating of garments with leather, termed *szironyozás*, by the Hungarians (examples of it are seen on the *szur*, a mantle with sleeves cut all in one with the bodice) shows the influence of the Asiatic horsemen. The term 'magyar sleeve' is probably derived from the type of sleeve seen on the *szür*. Magyar, or mares' milk drinkers, was the name of the people later known as Hungarians.

In Poland, the sheepskin coat decorated with braid and cut coloured leather shapes and worn particularly by the Tatra people shows a similar influence. This feeling for clear-cut shapes may have led later to the *Wycinanki*, or paper cuts for which Poland is famed.

Some of the designs found on the clothes of the Achal-Tekke Turcomen women, embroidered in green, dark red and blue silk, show similar designs, but these derive probably from a later date than the Mongol invasions, possibly during the Turkish triumphs, but they all came from a common root.

The embroideries on the dress of Dalmatia show strong Turkish influence. The clear-cut lines and the counter-change effects are similar to some embroidered decorations worked by the Golds of Siberia, who applied ornamental designs of dyed carp skin to the surface of their garments.

In Bosnia, after the Turkish occupation in the fourteenth century, much Oriental influence was evident. The opaskes, pieces of un-tanned hide laced from the pointed toes to the ankles, formed shoes. Breast plates made entirely of engraved silver coins were not unlike the jewellery worn in the time of Sigurkakhiti-Bega, mother of the great Kubla Khan.

The Renaissance in Europe and the study of the past made men consider their clothes and furnishings and in Italy especially, the princes and dukes vied with one another in pageantry. Their serving men and women were dressed in clothes designed by a master artist, and these gradually became the property of the servants and were handed down from one generation to another. The peasants realised the value of the beautiful materials and protected their costumes with false sleeves, cuffs and protective aprons, so that the present peasant costumes are somewhat removed from the original con-ception of the artist. Yet despite this, these costumes are different from those of other countries and retain the rich Renaissance influence.

Italy led in the styles of Europe, other countries followed, and fashions were created and costume at last *became* an art and a subject for study. In the sixteenth century Baron Siegmund Von Herbernstein visited several courts and published a book of woodcuts showing the various costumes he had seen. In 1562 the Italian engraver Enea Vico tried to depict the costumes of the globe. In 1580 Boissard published a very interesting book on costume. Certain outstanding features of costume were thus seen by men and women of other countries and the fashionable styles were imitated. Gradually one country took the premier position in leading fashion and was quickly copied, so that the distinctions in dress of the various cultured classes in Europe ceased during the sixteenth century.

In isolated places, highlands and islands, the peasants, through inaccessibility or hardship, preserved their old garments and so developed a national or provincial costume. These date usually from the sixteenth or seventeenth centuries. The costumes, often of great beauty, were handed from one generation to another and so the old styles were preserved and worn sometimes daily but usually only on festive occasions.

Following upon the invasion and conquest of a country new costumes and materials were introduced by the invaders. Thus in South America we find many styles based on Spanish costume. Later, when missionary work was developed, many native people abandoned their own beautiful costume to wear a version of European dress, but they wore it with a distinction and decorativeness adding ideas of their own and lending to it an unusual charm. Amongst the less civilised or industrialised people, costume is particularly decorative. The craftsmanship, though sometimes crude, is forceful and original in design. The head-dress is emphasised and was originally fashioned to give the wearer a feeling of power and also to strike fear into his enemies as well as a protection from the sun. The Kalinga head-dress from the Philippine Islands and the coiffure of a Fulah woman from French Guinea are masterpieces of design.

The ornamentation of the body by cicatrisation, tattoo or clay often reveals great artistry and a highly developed sense of pattern. Primitive materials, bamboos, rattans, birds' feathers, fish skin, shells, metal beads and clay are used as ornaments, often with more dexterity, native craftsmanship and decorative results than some of the elaborately produced materials of the more civilised people.

When surveying the costumes of other countries it seems strange that England, a country with so much tradition, is without a national costume. Indeed, foreign artists have shown Englishmen with a roll of material and shears in their hands in search of a national costume. But if there is not one distinctive national dress, England has many curious forms of costume with a long tradition, perhaps the oldest being the smock which has been worn since Saxon time by country folk. These were mainly of home-spun flax and wool, cut on simple, oblong lines and decoratively stitched. The motifs of design in the smocking suggest the trade of the wearer; pigman, ploughman, dairyman, shepherd and so forth, and different colours were worn in different counties.

The fishermen of England also wore a distinct type of dress. By their knitted designs, their jerseys and guernseys suggest the fishing village or part of the coast from whence the wearer comes. The traditional coster costume is worthy of note. The costermonger's pearlie suit covered by decorative patterns outlined with pearl buttons is not very far removed from some of the decorations in smeared clay with which natives covered their bodies: there is the same sense of balance and rhythm and the play of light against dark. The buttons are sometimes of pearl, sometimes of glass, and if of the latter the symbols of the " Road to Ruin," wine, women and song—the horse, dog, glass and women, are often engraved on the surface. The costumes are now only worn for festive occasions.

There are many ways in which the costumes in this book could have been arranged. Ethnographically, although this would have proved difficult, or under continents, are perhaps the most obvious classifications, but after careful consideration the most convenient way for a book which is intended to be used for reference seems to be a simple alphabetical order arranged under countries, with examples of ancient and historic costume at the end of the book.

A SWEDISH DECORATIVE MOTIF

WORLD COSTUMES

ABYSSINIA.   Abyssinian man wearing long robe and shawl.

ABYSSINIA. The men wear long shirts reaching over their trousers. Round the shoulders a shama or shawl is worn. The women wear skirts or robes, sometimes richly embroidered and occasionally covered with necklaces of beautiful workmanship.

WEST AFRICA, SOUTHERN NIGERIA. Below is an illustration of a dress once worn by a girl attendant on a nature image. Her hair is shaved above the forehead and then tightly plaited, and finally decorated with feathers. Shell and metal necklaces cover the chest and bracelets show off the beautifully shaped hands. **The** skirt is of native bark cloth.

The man wears a beautiful cloak of hand-woven West African cotton, richly embroidered in a native design.

NIGERIA

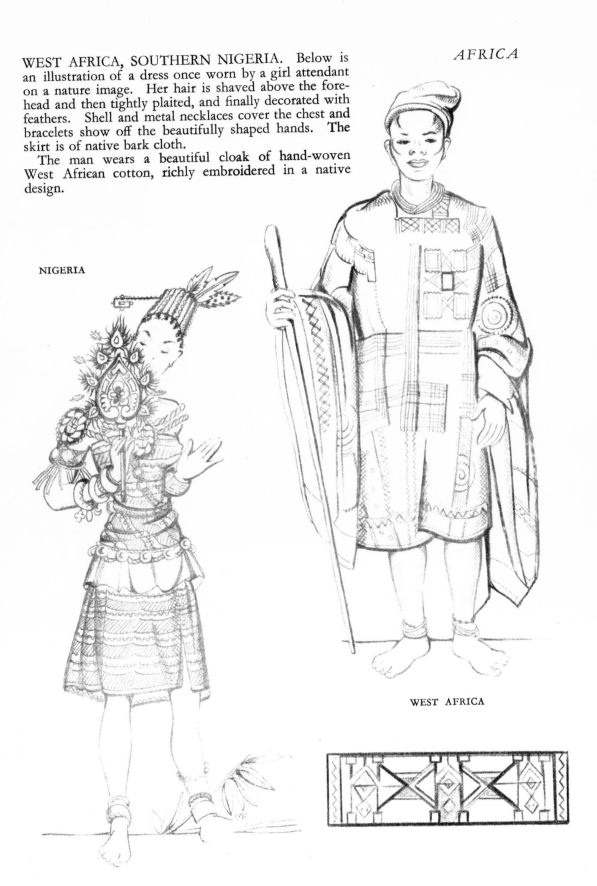

WEST AFRICA

NATAL. The Kaffir woman below, who comes from near Natal, wears a kilt-like skirt and a girdle of shells and beads. The hair is dragged back and moulded into a high standing cone. Sometimes a piece of cloth is twisted and worn tilted over the forehead.

GHANA. The woman above wears a brightly printed cotton drapery, heavy necklaces and bracelets of pale gold and aggry beads.

SUDAN. The woman wears her hair tightly plaited in the manner of the Early Egyptian head-dress. A long robe covers the body and is draped over the head.

MADAGASCAR. The girl to the right wears a variation of the native lama, a long rectangle of cloth thrown over the shoulder and wrapped round the body. Styles of hairdressing alter in different districts.

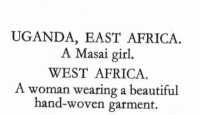

UGANDA, EAST AFRICA.
A Masai girl.
WEST AFRICA.
A woman wearing a beautiful
hand-woven garment.

ALBANIA. The Albanian female peasant costume sometimes has a small round hat with scarf hanging down the back. The robe is full and ankle length. The bodice is covered by a bolero. The leather shoes have curled-up toes.

The man's hat is round, his coat short, and a shaggy sheepskin covers his shoulders. His trousers are full and bound to the knee by puttees.

AMERICAN INDIANS OF THE SIOUX TRIBE.

They wear woollen dresses, thickly fringed and appliquéd. Their leggings are of buckskin and their moccasins are finely decorated.

AMERICAN INDIANS. This young unmarried girl of the Hopi Indians wears her hair in big puffs to symbolise the pumpkin flower, emblem of chastity. Married women wear long plaits representing the fruitful ears of corn.

AMERICAN INDIANS OF THE
NORTH-WEST. The woman wears
a large decorative blanket over her
shoulders, while the man has a magnificent head-dress of feathers.

ANATOLIA, now a province of
Turkey. The decorative dress of
this woman is long and full with
a shawl-like head-dress.

ARABIA. The Arab woman has perfect grace. Her loose robe is covered by material which can be draped in various ways.

ARABIA. This Arab wears white cotton twisted to form a turban. A long loose robe is covered by a bernouse.

ARMENIA. The designs on the woman's tunic coat show Persian influence.
Native jewellery is worn, and leather shoes with pointed toes. The head-dress
varies from a woven cap, small turban to coin-covered band, and draped scarf.
The men wear caps, turbans or astrakhan hats, long or short full trousers, pointed
leather shoes, thick coats and decorative waist scarves.

ASSAM. A Mishmi girl wears a patterned magyar jacket and short trousers. In her ear-lobes are decorative bamboo ear-plugs.

AUSTRALIAN ABORIGINES. Their decorations are
drawn with charcoal and edged with down. The arm-
lets round the upper arm are decorated with fur of
animals. On the floor is a native drum.

ÖTZAL   MÖLTEN   GRODEN

AUSTRIA. In Tyrol peasant dresses are worn on gala occasions. Embroidery is usually red on a white ground, and a favourite emblem or decoration is a small heart shape. The skirts are very full and often of printed fabric. Various forms of head-dress are worn in the different districts.

SALZBURG : HALLEIN   STEIERMARK : LEOBEN

AUSTRIA. Two male costumes from Tyrol. The costumes are richly embroidered. In the colour illustration on the opposite page the man's coat follows the lines of a seventeenth-century full-skirted riding-coat, his short trousers braided and held with a wide ornamented leather belt.

AUSTRIA: TYROL

AUSTRIA.   Lace and tatting are frequently used on the
costumes.   Jewellery is not too obvious, sometimes a
large brooch, a fürtuchsklemmer, is worn in the blouse.

C

BOLIVIA. The climate conditions the dress. The
people wear warm homespuns woven from the wool
of the llama or vicugna. The Aymara women wear
soft felt hats, and the Quichua women favour silver
spoons in the hair and on the dress.

BORNEO. The warrior youths of some of the tribes
in this country dress up, and on feast days the Dayak
men wear magnificent loin cloths of cotton or bark cloth,
girdles of metal discs, shoulder scarves and feathered
head-bands.

BORNEO. *From the top:* 1. a Lirong warrior; 2. a Klemantan woman; 3. Lirong girl; 4. a warrior.

The Dayak woman wears a ceremonial dress with corselet of rattans to which are fastened coins and rings. The hair is twisted into a knot and held in place with flowers.

BURMA. The man wears a cotton jacket, cotton shorts and a printed silk skirt and turban. The child is dressed in the same manner as an adult. Her coat is cotton and her skirt printed silk.

BURMA. The woman's long straight skirt is sometimes of cotton instead of the lovely Burmese silk. This is worn with a loose cotton jacket. Flowers are twisted into the rather severe hair style.

LAHU   TAUNGYOS

BURMA. Many tribes to the north of Burma wear picturesque costumes. The Lahu girl on the left wears an indigo robe frogged with red and white. Round her neck is a decorative silver boss.

The man wears a simple jacket of Chinese cut, and the woman on the right, from the Taungyos tribe, long trousers and a magyar skirt.

BURMA. A Lihsaw woman from the hilly country,
wearing a dark blue dress of thick material trimmed
with red froggings, a seed belt and silver torques round
the neck. Her belt is made of seeds. Another Lihsaw
woman is shown opposite. The woman on her right
wears a dyed indigo skirt and blouse with scarlet
appliqué. The circular head-dress denotes that she is
unmarried.

BURMA

CAMBODIA. The national costume
had a straight piece of material gathered round the waist and so fastened to
form a loose trouser-like skirt. The
bodice was covered by a straight embroidered jacket or a large coloured
draping which left the shoulders and
arms bare.

CEYLON. The Kandyan chiefs on a day of festival wrap many yards of fine silk or muslin round their waists and hold the cloth in position with an embroidered belt. Pointed shoes are worn and a curious shaped hat complete this handsome costume of white and gold. Women generally wear the long sari which can have the end draped over the head in a variety of ways according to the district.

CEYLON. A dancer, wearing a short flounced skirt,
turban, and bead chains on the chest.

CHINA. Long Magyar dresses are
worn by the Chinese women. The
little girl is in festive attire wearing a
beautifully embroidered silk kimona
dress and trousers.

CZECHOSLOVAKIA. The man wears high boots, with wide white linen fringed trousers and thick frieze coat. The woman in the front, more decorative than her sister, shows all her glorious skill as a needlewoman in golden yellow embroidery on a homespun blouse, the bodice is close fitting and the skirt, butcher blue embroidered in white and trimmed with lace.

CZECHOSLOVAKIA

CZECHOSLOVAKIA. The woman with a small Slovak boy is from Moravia.
The woman's skirt is short and bordered with cross stitch. The small boy
wears wide-legged homespun trousers sometimes fringed. Examples of the
elaborate embroidery on costume will be seen in the Moravian couple opposite.

CZECHOSLOVAKIA: MORAVIA

CZECHOSLOVAKIA. Carpathian Ruthenia. The Ruthenians have many beautiful costumes. The main feature is the long sheepskin coat. The quaint head-dress of the woman is worn over a twisted kerchief. Both men and women wear thick puttees round the leg. The broad belt is an essential part of the man's costume.

DENMARK. National costume is not often worn, but when it is, the men wear neat-fitting breeches buttoned at the knee, home knitted shoe and buckle shoes, trimmed jackets with metal buttons and stocking caps. The women wear bonnets and jackets over tight-fitting corsages and ankle-length skirts covered by neat aprons. The pleated apron the small girl wears is a modified form of ancient Danish costume.

DANISH DESIGNS

D

DUTCH EAST INDIES
now *INDONESIA*

Javanese women have attractive features
and graceful figures. They wear a short
thin robe, over which is a long garment.
Covering this is a sleeved coat brightly
coloured and often interwoven with gold
and silver threads. A *slendang* is draped
over the hair.

JAVA

EGYPT. A familiar figure is the water-carrier with his baggy trousers and indigo shirt of thin cotton.

The Arab girl's robe is loose and flowing and a cotton square covers her head.

ECUADOR. This native wears the beautiful Indian poncho made from hand woven material. Some of the finest ponchos are made from wool from the Highlands round Quito. The hat is a kind of sombrero.

ESTHONIA. The Esthonia costume, when worn on
festive occasions, is very decorative. The woman from
the Petseri district wears heavy silver trinkets. The
sleeves of the blouse are unusual, being dark insertion
worked with light embroidery.

FINLAND. Traditional costume is gradually dying out, but when worn on festive days consists of a long gathered skirt with full-sleeved blouse, patterned apron and head square. Reds and blues predominate and the patterns are usually geometric.

FORMOSA (Province of China). This Formosan native wears a short coat, shorts and waist cloth, a decorative necklace and a coolie hat. The Atayal woman of Formosa wears a shirt-like jacket, and a square of cloth woven of China grass with geometrical design in red, blue and black. Her head-dress is tied in a curious manner, and elaborate earrings complete the costume.

FRANCE. Costumes worn on gala occasions differ according to the district. This Norman peasant wears a calf-length skirt and a bright blue apron gathered to the waist, an embroidered blouse and a cross-over shawl. The head-dress is very decorative and is of lace and muslin.

FRANCE. Bordeaux peasant women wear a cross-over patterned shawl, a pannier skirt and covering apron. The men wear tall hats, sometimes of straw, white shirts and long trousers.

PYRENEES   AUVERGNE   BOURBONNAIS

FRANCE. The Pyrenean peasant wears the typical smock, loose trousers and beret which one associates with French workmen and which occur in many other parts of France. The woman of Auvergne wears her printed shawl drooping from the shoulders, while the Bourbonnais peasant has an attractive little bonnet, sometimes sabots, a striped blouse and full skirt covered by an apron.

FRANCE. Breton women wear full-skirted dresses with fitting bodices and neat little bonnets set well back upon the head. A variation of the style shows a large winged collar and a wide starched head-dress.

BLACK FOREST. Costumes are very gay and are worn mainly on special occasions. The general outline for women's dress follows the usual full skirt, worn over several petticoats, the corset, the bodice, or *leibli*, an apron and head covering. The men wear thick woollen stockings, knee-length trousers, waist-coats, short hip-length outer jackets or a long knee-length coat. The hat is of thin felt, flat brimmed and round or tall crowned. The umbrella is a favourite addition to the costume in this part of Germany.

BLACK FOREST The neat-fitting bodice has a full
skirt which is covered by a large apron. The small
loose pocket is usually attractively embroidered.

GERMANY: BLACK FOREST

HESSE-NASSAU. The costume which is worn on gala days has a rather quaint head-dress and a short knee-length skirt worn over several petticoats. This dress has a rather strange appearance when worn by elderly women.

BAVARIA

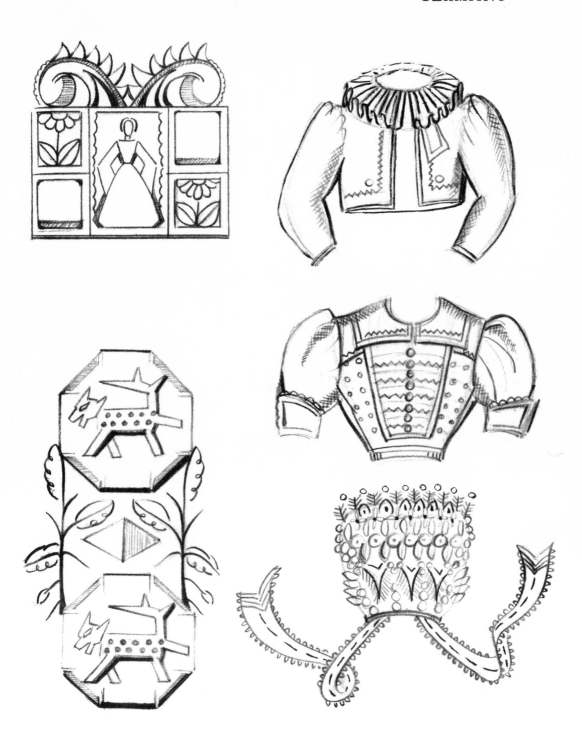

DETAILS OF ORNAMENT AND DECORATION

E

GREECE. The women of Greece cover their heads with small round caps and finely woven veils or headscarves. The blouse is worn under a jacket which is often embroidered. The skirt is long.

The wedding attire of a Greek peasant bride is often richly embroidered with gold, and coin necklaces are worn.

GREECE. The gala costume of some of the
men shows a short pleated kilt, red leather shoes
with pom-poms on the toes, a short jacket and
fez cap.

GREENLAND. The dress of the Eskimos is controlled by climatic
conditions. Trousers are common to both sexes, sometimes the
man wears a hooded garment of bird skins. A loose cotton vest
goes over this. The trousers are of sealskin and the boots and socks
of the same with the fur turned inside. The women wear similar
jackets with high collars of dog skin over decorative bead collars. In
the back of the coat is a small pouch to hold the baby. The
trousers are ornamented with decorative leather bands.

GREENLAND. The women's garments are often of sealskin and sometimes appliquéd or decorated with the soft skin of the eider duck.

HOLLAND. The Volendam woman's peasant costume is distinctive with its attractive Dutch bonnet of lace. The dress is often in butcher blue, the hip piece being of a different material, striped or checked, the yoke also is in another colour. On the feet *klompen,* or wooden shoes. The man has full trousers, a double-breasted coat and soft round cap.

HOLLAND. This man of Zealand wears the typical costume of the Netherland peasant, worn now on gala occasions. The trousers are full, the waistcoat double-breasted, the coat short and wide, and the cap peaked. The woman has a tight-fitting bodice, puffed sleeves, full skirt, sometimes kilted to show the petticoats underneath. The attractive pancake hat is tied on the head over a little lace bonnet, sometimes a winged cap is worn.

ZEALAND. A woman wearing the attractive winged cap, high neckline and full skirt and wooden shoes of this district.

HUNGARY. The traditional peasant costume of Hungary worn on festive occasions is very decorative. The cowherd from the great plains wears a beautiful sleeved cloak decorated with coloured leather bands and motifs. This is worn slung across the chest, and on the head is a hard round felt hat.

HUNGARY. The men wear
dark-coloured aprons covered
with bright embroidery. Their
shirts have embroidery on their
wide cuffs.

HUNGARY. The women show their industry in embroidery on their own and their men folks' clothes. The skirts of their own dresses are sometimes ankle- or knee-length and worn over several petticoats. The blouses have puffed sleeves or long full ones. The frill on the waist is occasionally stiffened with cardboard. The apron is woven or heavily embroidered.

NEPAL is an independent kingdom, adjacent to India, and for convenience the costumes of the country, shown on this page and on page 89, are included along with other costumes of the great subcontinent of India. The Nepalese dress is warm and follows the usual magyar lines with cross-over bodice. They wear small round hats and thick felt boots. The women wear ankle-length robes, sometimes tucked up when working in the rice fields.

INDIAN DANCERS

NEPAL. These decorative costumes are from Nepal. The girl on the left wears the usual cross-over magyar type of robe in thick material, while the one on the right is in the old court dress and wears a curious tasselled hat, full trousers and fitting coat.

CENTRAL INDIA. One of the forest tribes. The man wears a small round cap to protect his head against the strong sun, a simple cotton jacket and shorts.

The woman covers her head, too. Her robe is knee-length, an unusual feature.

INDIA. The grace of the costume of the women of
India is famed. The beautiful materials and exquisite
colourings of the saris are the envy of Western women.

TAMIL. A Hindu bride in the Tamil country dressed
in wedding finery.

INDIA. A Nautch dancing-girl wearing beautiful, finely spun garments—their whole effect lending grace to the dance.

F

KASHMIR. The Chamba woman of Kashmir wears a curious little hat over her severe hair style. Under her short frilled jacket she has a long robed dress often of patterned material. The necklaces are of roughly cut stones.

INDIA. Worthy of note is the costume worn by a fakir of the Sohagia order. These men adopt women's clothes.

IRELAND. The costume is very simple, but is worn only on festive occasions, although the everyday attire of many country women is very similar. The man wears a jaunty hat, a twisted stock and an eighteenth-century style jacket. The woman has a blouse, a wide skirt in home-spun worn over several petticoats, and a shawl on her head.

MOLISE   CALABRIA   SARDINIA

ITALY. Peasant costumes, which are worn on gala days, are rather different
from those of other countries. They have the appearance of having been
designed by an artist—which many of them were in their original form.
The materials used are linens, woollens, lace, brocades and velvets. The
aprons and sleeves in many cases were used in the first instance to protect
the rich material of the dress. Later these separate sleeves and aprons
assumed decorative form and became a permanent part of·the costume.

CALABRIA   SARDINIA

CAMPANIA   SICILY   ABRUZZI

ITALIAN DESIGNS

JAMAICA

JAMAICA. The cotton gown of the native woman is usually scrupulously clean and laundered, a coloured handkerchief is draped round her shoulders, and a handkerchief turban-wise binds up her hair, but European and American styles are worn most of the time.

JAPAN. Western dress is worn to a great extent in Japan, but when the national costume is worn, the beautiful kimona is the distinctive note. The kimona for everyday wear in the summer time is of cotton, called a yukata. For visiting, this is replaced by one of silk worn over an under robe. The garment is held in position by the obi or waistband. The *haori*, or overcoat, is worn over the kimona. In winter a wadded kimona, named a water-ire, is worn for warmth. Japanese labourers wear dark-coloured trousers and a knee-length coat, termed a happi coat, and wooden clogs.

JAPAN

JAPAN.   Japanese men wear a wide-sleeved, cross-over robe cut on magyar lines with a sash round the waist.

JAPAN. Sometimes the women's cross-over robe is
worn bunched round the waist.

KOREA. The women wear an outer cloak with full
sleeves and draped skirt termed a chang-ot. This is
of thin green silk and was at one time used as an eye-veil
when pulled up over the neck. Under this is a voluminous ankle-length skirt gathered round the waist by
a broad belt and covered by a short zouave-like jacket of
cotton.

KOREA. In the costume worn by the men, perhaps the most unusual feature is the hat, rather like a Welsh hat in shape. It is tied under the chin by strings. A loose kimona style of coat is worn over baggy trousers. The shoes are of thick felt with turned-up toes.

KURDISTAN. This woman wears a tall head-dress, the scarf draped round the chin and over the shoulders. The long robe is covered by a hip-length jacket bound with a woven waist belt.

KURDISTAN. This man wears a rough shirt, trousers, sometimes printed or woven, a fringed waistband and top boots.

LABRADOR. Eskimos from Labrador. The women
carry their babies in the hoods of their sealskin dickies.
Shirts, thick woollen stockings and sealskin boots are
worn.

G

LAPLAND. The men wear thick shirts, woollen or skin trousers, covered by knee-length tunics, which are sometimes belted with belts of beautiful workmanship. Tall six-gored hats, and boots of reindeer skin complete the costume.

The women's dress is very similar, only several petticoats are worn under the skirt and the garments are sometimes beautifully decorated in tin threads which give the appearance of silver.

Lapp women on the coast are striking in their white or grey woollen frocks bordered with scarlet and blue and gathered by brightly coloured sashes.

LATVIA. The peasant garments which are worn on gala days are mainly of homespun. The skirts are full and voluminous. The blouses are covered by short jackets of hip length. A scarf covers the head except on special days when a more decorative circlet or crown is worn. The stockings are thick and hand-knitted. The jewellery, which is often of silver or amber, is beautiful in design. The men wear tunic coats, long trousers in or over leather boots, and peaked caps.

MEXICO. The Mexican Indian woman of Tehuantepec wears the distinctive *huipil* head-dress. This represents the frock of a baby rescued from the coast long ago. The child was said to bring good luck to its rescuers. The dress is worn like a huge bonnet with the sleeves and collar hanging down the back. Another example of the *huipil* head-dress will be seen on the page opposite.

MEXICO

MEXICO. The Mexican wears his loose white cotton trousers belted with braid at the waist, his zarape flung over one shoulder and an old sombrero on his head. Another example of male costume will be seen on page 117. Note particularly the brightly dyed woollen zarape and the tight-fitting riding breeches.

MONGOLIA. Male and female dress is very similar. The coat is of thick material, very long and with exceptionally wide sleeves ending in large cuffs which sometimes serve the purpose of a muff. The man's hat has a fur brim and ear-flaps, the woman's has a conical crown covered by silk and mounted with a decorative glass ball. Three tassels hang down the back. The boots have turned-up toes and are of thick felt. The woman on page 121 wears a winged head-dress through which her hair is threaded and hangs in thick plaits on either side. Her companion wears a thick winter overcoat of silk, with wide cuffs into which he can push his hands. The small girl with them wears the cross-over bodice, so typical of all Mongolian costumes.

MONGOLIA

MOROCCO. The Moorish lady shows her wealth in the beautiful brocade robe she wears covered by a wide-sleeved garment of striped silk. The head is draped and necklaces hang round the neck. The leather slippers are exquisitely tooled and painted. The man wears a plain white-sleeved cotton robe over trousers, and his head and shoulders are covered by a form of the hooded jellab.

NORWAY. The woman comes from Hardanger, famed for its exquisite embroidery. The *skaut*, or head-dress, is of gophered linen. The man comes from the northern regions. The little girl in the foreground has a cap of scarlet embroidered in yellow, and her short, sleeveless jacket, also scarlet, is worn with an embroidered vest over a white blouse. Her skirt is blue. The child on the left is from Hallingdal: she wears a loose pinafore dress with embroidered yoke, over a white high-necked blouse.

PERSIA. The old costumes are gradually dying
out, but in some of the nomadic tribes the
trousers and embroidered coats and turbaned
head-dresses of the women can still be seen.
The man, sketched, wears an astrakhan hat, long
loose trousers covered by a short striped shirt,
bound round the waist with a scarf. The shoes,
sometimes of cotton, are termed givas.

PERU. The Quichuas, one of the original tribes of Peru, wear straw or felt hats, wool shoulder blankets and rough hide shoes or sandals.

PHILIPPINE ISLANDS. The Tinguian woman at top left wears a wrap-over cotton skirt and jacket. Her hair which is knotted is held in place with strands of beads. The Kalinga woman with her wears a decorative costume with thick bead necklaces. The couple shown above, with their curious head-dresses, are from the Ifuguos race.

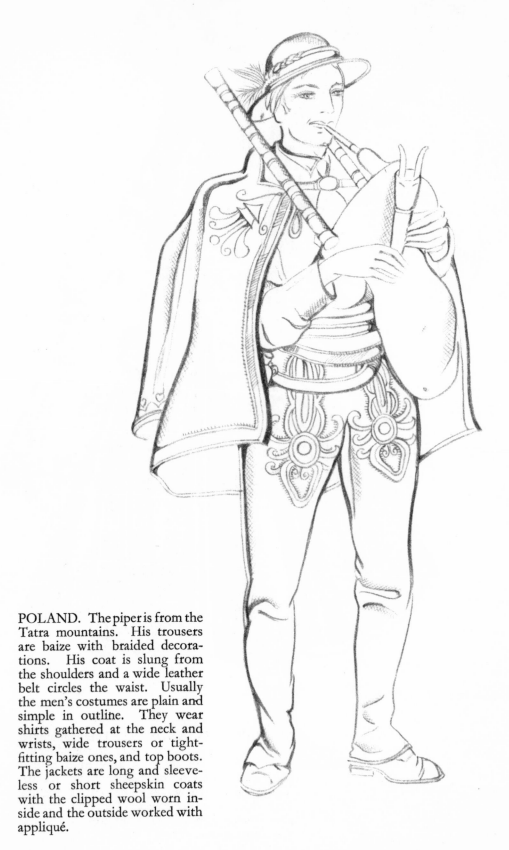

POLAND. The piper is from the Tatra mountains. His trousers are baize with braided decorations. His coat is slung from the shoulders and a wide leather belt circles the waist. Usually the men's costumes are plain and simple in outline. They wear shirts gathered at the neck and wrists, wide trousers or tight-fitting baize ones, and top boots. The jackets are long and sleeve-less or short sheepskin coats with the clipped wool worn inside and the outside worked with appliqué.

POLAND

POLAND. The woman is from the Lowicz district and wears a colourful striped dress, full-sleeved blouse and head-square. The girl on page 129 is from Holm. Her beads are of amber, glass and coral.

PORTUGAL. Portuguese peasant costumes are not very elaborate. The men sometimes wear rough frieze coats, stocking caps and sheepskin leggings.

In the group of three figures, the man, from Oporto, wears a plain shirt, coloured waistcoat with sleeves and a sleeveless over-jacket. The trousers are long and tight-fitting. The central figure is from Vianna do Castello, the gaily applied apron is a notable feature. The woman on the right is from Leiria. The head-dress and thick drapery are in black, the skirt in dark material with a hem of red, while the blouse is in amber.

PORTUGAL

PORTUGAL. The shepherd above has a frieze jacket and close-fitting breeches. His companion from Vianna do Castello has a shawl embroidered in satin stitch.

ROUMANIA. The woman wears a
winter jacket over a long robe. On her
head she wears a veil of thin muslin or
fine linen.

ROUMANIA. This peasant costume has a blouse of fine hand-woven linen, beautifully embroidered in red and black on the top of the sleeves and down the front. A long straight skirt of dark material has a covering apron of striped hand-woven fabric kilted round the waist. A thin embroidered veil drapes the head.

H

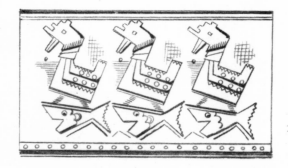

ROUMANIA. The top couple show the jolly round hat decorated with flowers worn by the man and the unusual short embroidered wrap-over apron. The woman's head-dress is a floral crown and her short sheepskin jacket is decorated with coloured leather.

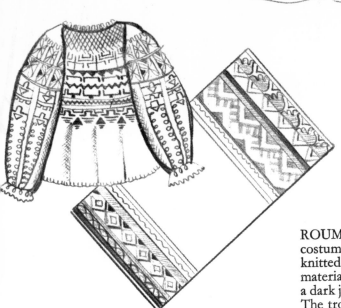

ROUMANIA. The girl wears a winter costume, hooded, and with thick hand-knitted stockings bound with strips of material. The man's shirt is covered by a dark jacket and a sleeveless leather coat. The trousers are of the same material, or baize, and worn inside high boots.

The blouse and towel-ends in the small sketches show the skill of the Roumanian needlewoman.

GEORGIA, CAUCASUS. The costumes worn on
gala days by the Russians were very varied and very
beautiful. These peasants are from the Caucasus.

RUSSIA. These women wearing the gala costume of a country district outside Moscow have lapots on their feet made of birch bark. Their printed cotton tunics show separate sleeves which are decorated at the shoulders with embroidery. The man has high boots, a tunic over his trousers, and a peaked cap.

RUSSIA.   This woman is from Riazon.   Her elaborate
tunic has beautiful shoulder embroidery.   The high head-
dress covers her severe hair style.

RUSSIA. These decorative costumes are worn by
peasants of Runa Island, in the Gulf of Riga.

RUSSIA. These costumes from Kiev show the woman's long loose robe covered by a sleeveless sarafan and thick coat, the girdle woven and fringed, and the boots made of thick felt.

The man has a shirt of linen, trousers of printed linen, and a homespun coat and high boots of leather.

SIBERIAN TARTARS

RUSSIA: SIBERIA. The costumes worn by the different races in Siberia are most varied. Of Mongolian origin the people wear thick garments of felt or skin decorated with geometric patterns. Their hats are of fur or felt. The coat of the man on page 145 is decorated with strips of coloured leather. The woman with him belongs to a more northern tribe; and the baby is from an Eastern Siberian tribe.

SCOTLAND. Perhaps one of the most picturesque costumes comes from Scotland's quaysides. The skirt of the fisherwomen is of dark or striped homespun, tucked and sometimes kilted to the waisted, revealing, striped or plain underskirts. Cardigans and jerseys and warm shawls complete the costume and show the industry and superb craftsmanship of the women.

SIAM. Two Siamese dancers from the traditional ballet based on the Ramayana, an early Sanscrit epic. Their lavish costumes of silk covered with gold and silver embroidery are sewn and fitted on to the dancers before each performance.

SIAM. A Siamese dancer in traditional dress. Gold and silver embroidered silk of a heavy quality and cotton robes.

The small sketches show some Siamese head-dresses.

SPAIN. The costumes worn on gala days are simple
but most becoming. The costume shown above is worn
by the women of Mercia. The wrap-over shawl, the full-
skirt and apron are often beautifully embroidered.

SPAIN. The flounced dress worn by the centre figure in the group is worn by a dancer from Granada. The figure on the left wears a comb and mantilla head-dress, a relic of the Eastern veil.

SWEDEN. This costume is from Skäne and shows the attractive pleated linen cap. The detailed drawings show winter mittens, a jewelled pendant, and an embroidered shirt. The man in the frontispiece to this book is from Dalarne, the central figure from Södermanland, and the women on the right from Lapland. The two women's costumes on page 155 are from Dalarne.

SWEDEN. The Swedish peasant costumes worn on
festive days, and in particular on Midsummer Eve, are
distinguished by their hand work either in weaving,
dyeing or embroidery. "Sloyd," or handicraft, is taught
in schools. Above is a typical example of Swedish costume. The girl on the left is from Insjon; the collar
and cap are embroidered and the waist girdle woven.

SWEDEN

SWEDISH FABRIC DESIGNS AND DECORATIONS

I

SWITZERLAND   Although every canton in Switzerland does not possess a special dress, some cantons have more than one. Generally local costumes date from the late seventeenth century. The central figure is from Valais, where there are many different costumes. The black cap of the Bernese peasant is of horsehair lace work, and on the right is a Seelisberg costume. This is mainly blue with a red corsage and yellow front.

SWITZERLAND

SWITZERLAND. A woman from Seelisberg wearing a wide decorative hat and an Appenzall peasant watch a little maiden from Berne. On the left is a design on printed wood.

TIBET. The couple here are from the Ladakhis tribe of Tibet. Their full-length robes are of silk on broadcloth, quilted or lined with fur. Their hats have furlined ear-flaps and their boots are of thick felt.

TIBET. The head-dress of the woman is a cane frame covered by strings of pearl beads studded with coral, turquoise and other uncut stones. The hair is drawn to the edge of the head-dress and hangs in two braids. The decorative amulet box to guard against the Evil-one is shown worn round the neck. The sleeves are extremely long, making a muff for the hands. The man wears a turned-up cap, sometimes of fur or felt—a knee-length tunic of thick material cut in magyar fashion, the boots are thick felt, sometimes decorated.

WALES. The national costume worn on gala days is very picturesque. The main feature of the women's costume is the tall crowned black hat, the dresses have full skirts, laced bodices, blouses and shawls which are usually in checks and stripes of vivid blacks, whites, reds and greens.

TURKESTAN

YUGOSLAVIA. There are many lovely styles in different localities. The buttons, beads, sequins and coins and the rich, thickly encrusted embroideries and gorgeous colourings make the Macedonian costumes outstanding from the rest of Yugoslavia.

All the drawings are of Macedonian costumes except the woman with the full baggy trousers: she is a Moslem and shows her attractive costume with its coin necklaces and kerchief head covering.

YUGOSLAVIA. This Macedonian couple wear a different style of costume. The man's trousers are tight-fitting and braided and are worn with a wide waist-band. His decorated waistcoat is worn over an embroidered shirt. The embroidery on the bodice of the girl's dress is in gold; her apron is richly embroidered.

YUGOSLAVIA

YUGOSLAVIA.   A small boy from Kupinovo and a
Macedonian woman wearing a costume with sequins.
beads and coins shining among coloured embroidery.

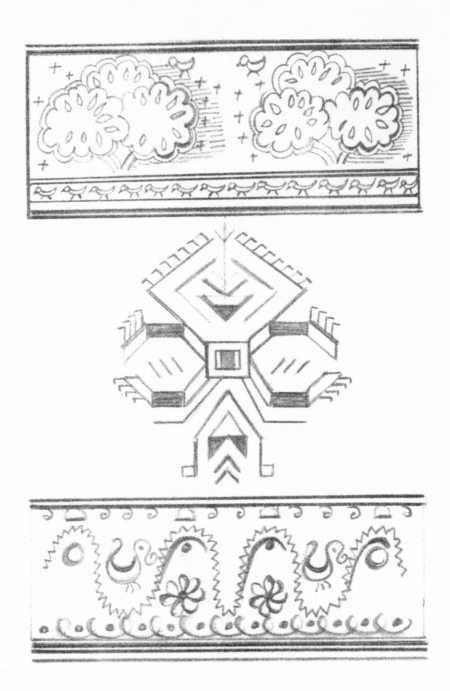

SPECIMENS OF YUGOSLAVIAN DESIGN

ANCIENT COSTUME

ANCIENT COSTUME

THE drawings on pages 173 to 175 illustrate ancient costumes which have influenced fashion through the ages. In some parts of Roumania the peasant costume shows little change since the days of the Dacians as portrayed in Trajan's column. Other peasant costumes, as in the case of Italy, show the glory of the fifteenth and sixteenth centuries when they were originally planned by a great artist as part of the pageantry of a wealthy overlord, and made in rich velvets and brocades. These costumes later became the property of the peasants, who added detachable sleeves, aprons and head-scarves to protect and preserve the exquisite materials.

Other peasant costumes, for instance the Swedish, show distinct eighteenth-century trends, although some date earlier, but we do know that interest in the costumes was taken in 1630 when Gustavus Adolphus in a proclamation had all the costumes and customs of his people noted.

The ancient costumes on page 173 show Egyptian dresses of fine linen with darned embroidered motifs. The Babylonian costume next is distinctive by reason of its fringes and braids.

The Hebrew woman shows the long linen or wool robe ornamented with gold work, a method described in the book of Exodus in the Bible.

Some Persian costumes of silk were of exquisite colour as they possessed the secret of the ancient Eastern dyes. Some of the Greeks wore finely draped clothes of wool or linen sometimes embroidered with golden spangles, needle-weaving or dyed by the resist process, which they appear to have understood.

On page 174 an Etruscan woman, of the non-Aryan tribe which was in Italy before the Romans, shows the garment of thick wool or linen decorated with spots and stars.

The Roman woman and the three in the group show the simple tunic covered by the toga, or as in the case of the women, the stola and palla.

The Byzantine dress was probably beautifully woven, as the luxury of the Eastern emperors and their courts created a demand for skilled craftsmen; the garment was possibly of silk because sericulture was introduced from Khotan at the time of Justinian. Byzantine dress can be seen to have influenced Russian styles, probably through the marriages of the princesses of the Imperial court with the Russians.

On page 175 the old Dacian costume, the forerunner of the Roumanian dress, is sketched, together with a Celt and a woman of Gaul.

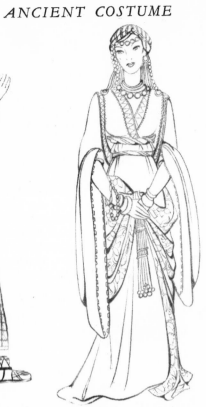

ANCIENT EGYPTIAN   BABYLONIAN   ANCIENT HEBREW

ANCIENT PERSIAN

EMBROIDERED COAT AND
FELT MITRE

CHLAMYS   DORIC CHITON   CHITON AND HIMATION

ANCIENT GREEK

ETRUSCAN

ROMAN
UNDERTUNIC, STOLA AND PALLA

TUNIC AND TOGA   ROMAN   CORSELET WITH KILT

BYZANTINE   TUNIC AND MANTLE   DACIAN

CELTIC
PLAID WOOLLEN TUNIC AND WOOLLEN CLOAK

ANCIENT GAUL
WOOLLEN AND LEATHER TUNIC,
BRONZE ORNAMENTS

ENGLISH COSTUME

ENGLAND has no traditional national costume, except perhaps the smock, which has been worn by the countrymen for hundreds of years and is still found made of strong unbleached linen with exquisite smocking on the yoke and cuffs.

But there is a wealth of design in the historical costumes of England and these, both in material and style, have influenced many European fashions. A brief survey of some of these fashions are sketched on pages 178 to 191. The Norman couple on page 178 show the costumes which we find so well illustrated in the Bayeux tapestry. Exaggerated sleeves were the main feature of women's dress, sometimes these were so long they were tied in knots. The men at the foot of the page illustrate that lovely period termed " Decorated " in English history, a colourful age when the influence of the crusades was evident, and heraldry appeared.

The women wore tight-fitting surcoats and the head was veiled. Fur became very much the vogue, and the medieval trade names for skins are still used in heraldry. Cloaks were lined with fur and dress often trimmed by it. Women wore one-piece garments cut to define the waist and covered by a wide arm-holed outer garment. Sometimes sleeves were laced on and often a dress had several pairs.

Materials of the best quality came from England, a beautiful woollen material termed scarlet was much used. German linens were rare and cottons from the East luxuries, cotton velvets came from Lucca and wool velvets from Venice and the Saracens brought silk weaving from Sicily. The first book on dyeing was published in Venice and the Dyers Company in London formed in 1472. Parti-coloured costumes were much favoured, dagging was fashionable, and curious turbaned headgear and beaver hats were worn.

The making of clothes became an art although tailors guilds had been established in many countries years before.

Shoes were ankle length with leather soles and laced sides. The legs were encased in hose which were laced on to the under hose. Women's garments became fitting to the figure and were laced or buttoned, and had full skirts. Albert Dürer's drawings show the beautiful lines of this period on the Continent.

Slashing was a feature introduced into dress. The undergarments were often revealed and showed attractive embroidery. Men's breeches took on exaggerated styles and were often padded or bombasted. Shoes were ox-jawed and rosetted, and ruffs grew in favour. Men's hair was cut short and beards were fashionable. Women sometimes had separate cuffs and sleeves to their dresses. The bodices were fitting and the necks décolleté, the skirts bell-shaped and showing an elaborate under-dress. The Stuart cap was much favoured.

The ruff grew in proportions on both men's and women's costumes, some were of lace and others of tatting. The important business was to starch them properly and this was taught for four pounds a lesson ; sometimes they were tinted with blue or yellow starch. Women's hair was dressed high, the square of the neck was filled in, bodices were elongated, and the farthingale was worn over a bolster-like padding. The bombasting in the men's breeches grew less and the garments were let down to the knee.

Cromwellian England was a land of contrasts. The gay colourful cavaliers contrasted with the sombre simplicity of the Puritans. The Cavalier men wore their hair long and curling. The ruff turned down and became a large lace Stuart collar. The breeches were without padding and finished at the knee with ribbon rosettes, the doublet was hip length, and stockings or strong boots were worn.

The women's costume was very elegant, the great hip pads were removed and the skirt fell in graceful folds. Pretty petticoats of satin, taffeta and silk trimmed with gold lace were worn.

The Puritans' dress followed the same outline but without the frills and in sombre colours.

Muffs became fashionable for both men and women, the peplum on the women's bodice descended. Men's doublets were lengthened until they became loose coats, knee-breeches and stockings were worn, the shirt sleeve fell in loose folds to the wrist where it ended in a ruff, collars gave place to cravats.

All the exaggerated styles of the Restoration had disappeared and a dignity in costume grew. The materials reflected the growth of Britain's power as a maritime nation ; silks, brocades, cottons and fine muslins from the East were used for dress fabrics.

Men wore colourful attire ; waistcoats embroidered in silks, tinsels and spangles ; buttons at the centre of the back held the full-skirted coat when riding. Heads were covered by wigs, the full-bottomed wig appearing first.

Gradually these wigs became inconvenient for men of action and smaller wigs were worn. These were powdered with rice-meal and wheat-meal. Women's hair styles became exaggerated, skirts began to be padded, then hooped over whalebone until their proportions became incongruous. The coat tails from the full skirts of the men were cut away later, and a three-cornered hat was worn or carried under the arm.

Colours began to change ; Perkin had made his discoveries with aniline and dyes and experiments in dyeing were beginning. Breeches were lengthened and had become rather like the trouser of to-day. The beaver hat became fashionable, dark-coloured waistcoats found favour, and the wig was discarded. The industrial changes taking place were reflected in the colouring and cut of the clothes. Women wore simple garments cut on Grecian lines and the minimum of under-clothing was worn. This led later to draperies, shawls and fichus for extra warmth, and the carrying of handbags.

French fashion journals had circulated since 1672 and French dolls wearing the latest styles had been sent to this country until the wars of Napoleon stopped them. People were very interested in dress and in the costumes of other countries. Women began to wear more petticoats and gradually to build over a steel and cane crinoline cage. Men wore long trousers and the jacket had achieved similar lines to the coat of to-day. Women's emancipation had begun, doors were opening to them in the professions and their dress accordingly became more suitable. The crinoline disappeared and the attractive bell-shaped skirt took its place together with the neat braided jacket, a forerunner of to-day's classic suit.

K

NORMAN

1350
GOWN, UNDER-TUNIC HOSE, AND SHOES

1350
LINEN WIMPLE, ROBE AND MANTLE

1400
SURCOAT AND COTE HARDIE

1450
HENNIN AND WIMPLE OVER NET CAULS,
PATTERNED OVER-DRESS AND UNDER-DRESS

CHAPERON TURBAN

1450
HOUPPELANDE, ROUNDLET WITH CHAPERON

1500

FELT HAT, JACKET AND ALTERNATING HOSE

1500

1550
WINGED CAP, SQUARE-NECKED ROBE,
SLASHED UNDER-SLEEVES

1550
BEAVER HAT, DOUBLET, TRUNK HOSE, SHOES AND ROSES

1600
FELT HAT, RUFF, STOMACHER, GOWN AND UNDER-GOWN

1600
DOUBLET AND TRUNK HOSE

1640
JACKET, SLASHED SLEEVES, BREECHES
AND LEATHER BOOTS

1650
CLOTH GOWN AND EMBROIDERED UNDER-GOWN

1650
PURITAN GOWN, COLLAR, CUFFS AND APRON OF LINEN

1675

COAT, CRAVAT AND SHIRT, RUFFLES,
BREECHES AND LEATHER SHOES

1675

1700
STOMACHER, SMALL PEPLUM, RUFFLES

1700
COAT, VEST, BREECHES, STOCKINGS, LEATHER SHOES
AND COCKED HAT CARRIED UNDER THE ARM

1780
FORMAL HEAD-DRESS POWDERED, GOWN RUCHED
AND GATHERED TO SHOW UNDER-GOWN.

1780
FLAT BEAVER HAT, WIG, COAT
AND BUCKSKIN TROUSERS.

PAGE 189

1800
BONNET, MUFF, PARASOL AND MUSLIN GOWN

1815
BEAVER HAT, CRAVAT, COAT, TROUSERS AND BOOT

1850

BONNET AND RIBBONS, COAT AND GOWN, WHILE THE MAN
WEARS CRAVAT, FLOWERED WAISTCOAT AND TIGHT TROUSERS

1900
FEATHERED HAT, LEG OF MUTTON SLEEVES,
BRAIDED JACKET AND SKIRT